WORLD OF SPORTS
GOLF

Published by Smart Apple Media
1980 Lookout Drive, North Mankato, Minnesota 56003

Photographs by Icon Sports Media (Robert Beck, John Biever, Jim Gund), Sports Gallery (Al Messerschmidt)

Design and production by EvansDay Design

LIBRARY OF CONGRESS CATALOGING-IN-PUBLICATION DATA

Frisch, Aaron.
Golf / by Aaron Frisch.
p. cm. — (World of sports)
Summary: Surveys the history, equipment, courses, techniques, and legendary players in the sport of golf.
ISBN 1-58340-161-X
1. Golf—History—Juvenile literature. [1. Golf.] I. World of sports (Mankato, Minn.).

GV968 .F75 2002
796.352—dc21 2002017709

First Edition
9 8 7 6 5 4 3 2 1

AARON FRISCH

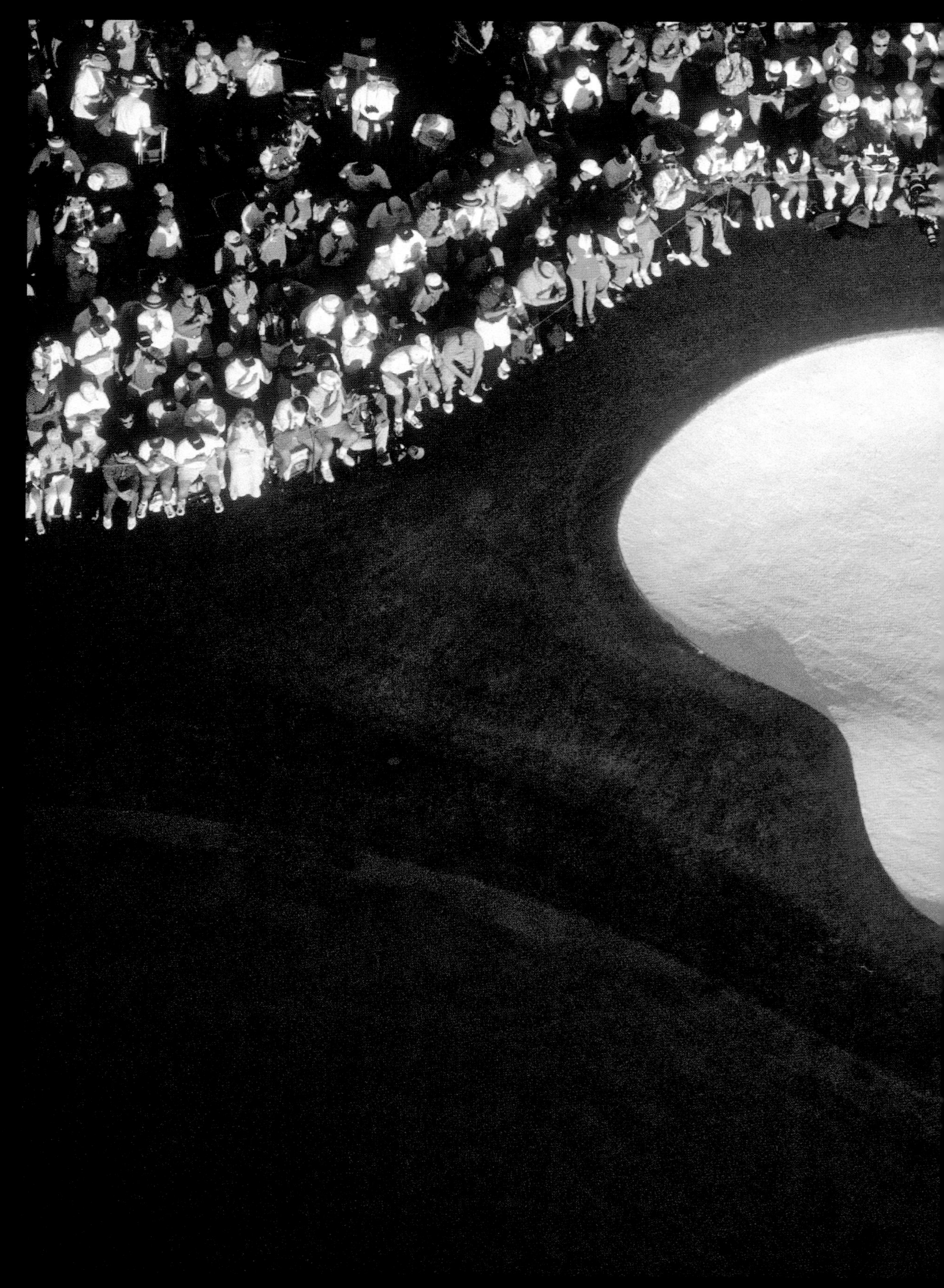

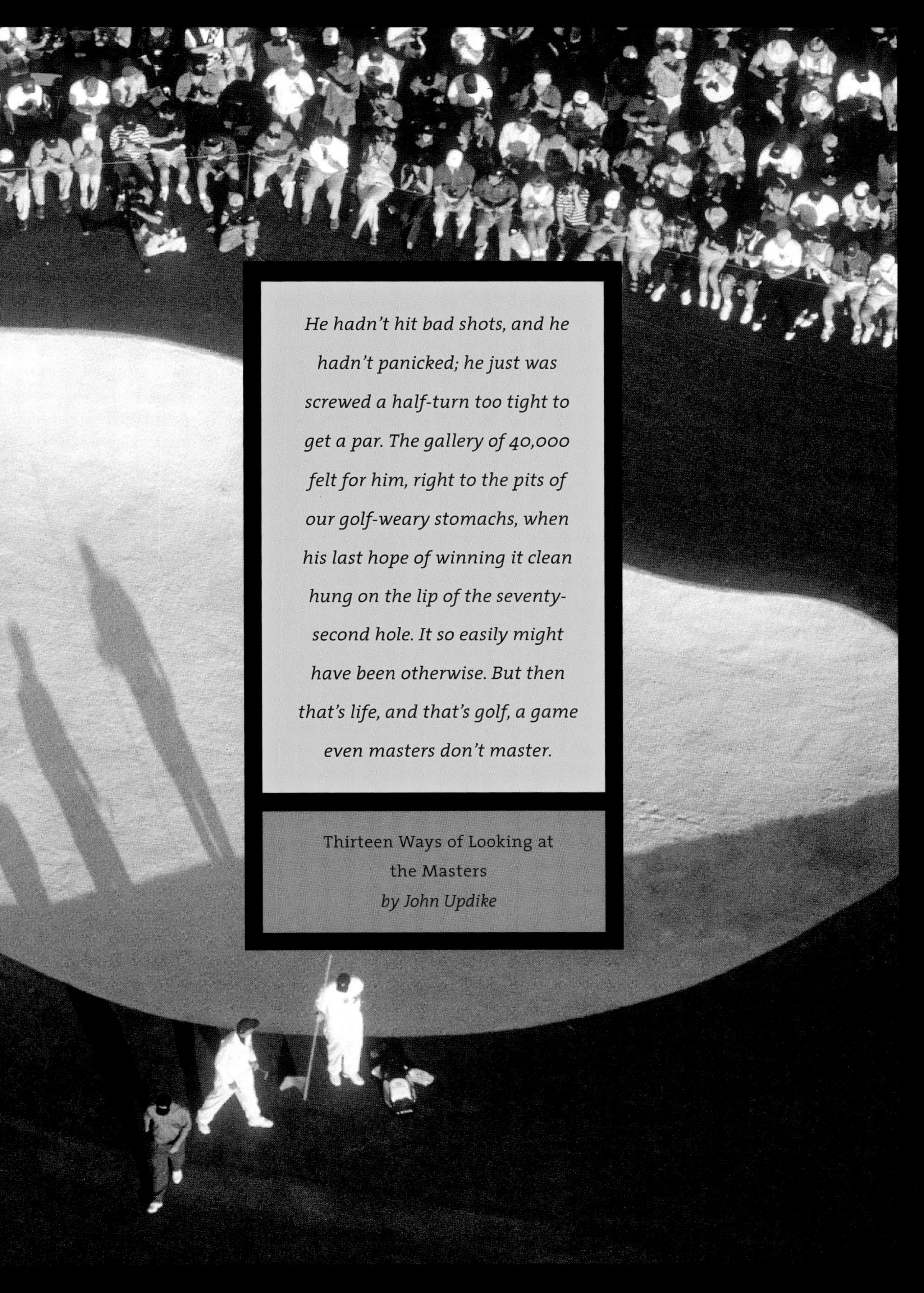

He hadn't hit bad shots, and he hadn't panicked; he just was screwed a half-turn too tight to get a par. The gallery of 40,000 felt for him, right to the pits of our golf-weary stomachs, when his last hope of winning it clean hung on the lip of the seventy-second hole. It so easily might have been otherwise. But then that's life, and that's golf, a game even masters don't master.

Thirteen Ways of Looking at the Masters
by John Updike

The Evolution of Golf

Golf seems like such a simple sport—knocking a small white ball around a grassy landscape into a bunch of holes in the fewest possible number of hits, or strokes. Yet it is actually an extremely challenging game, one that can be thrilling one moment and frustrating the next. Some people would agree with famous writer Mark Twain, who called it "a good walk spoiled." But for millions of others, few things in life offer such simple satisfaction as hitting a golf ball well.

King James IV of Scotland, an avid golfer, helped introduce the game to England in the early 1500s. He is among the earliest golfers about whom there is authentic evidence.

There's a lot to love about golf. It gives players a sense of power as they thwack a ball with a slender stick and watch it soar. It requires and develops patience and precision. It's a wonderful excuse to spend time outdoors on beautiful summer days, and a fine means of exercise. For these reasons and more, close to 40 million people around the world have become golfers.

Canon
Seoul '88

Golf originated in Scotland in the 1400s. The sport became so popular that the Scottish Parliament issued a decree on more than one occasion encouraging people to spend less time playing golf and more time practicing archery, a “useful” sport that could be used to defend the country in times of war.

But golf had already put down deep roots in Scotland, and people were unwilling to give it up. In 1744, the very first golf club, known as the Company of Gentleman Golfers, was founded in Edinburgh, Scotland. The club, which still exists, is today known as the Honorable Company of Edinburgh Golfers.

Ten years later, a group of golfers in St. Andrews, a town near Edinburgh, organized their own club. This club, called the Society of St. Andrews Golfers (today known as the Royal and Ancient Golf Club), did much to further the sport. It drew up a clear set

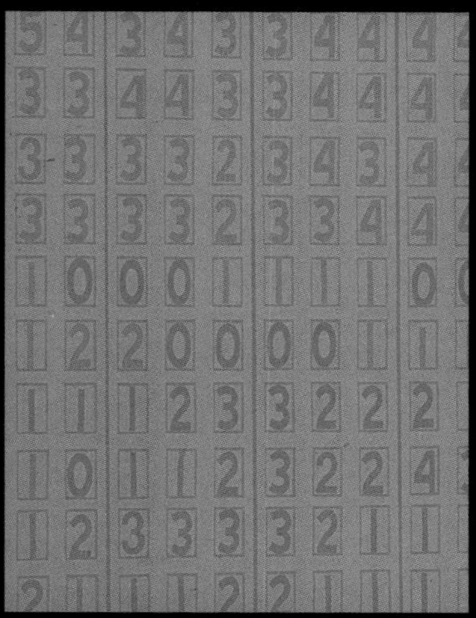

The famous Royal and Ancient Golf Club in Scotland, the country in which golf originated.

of rules, which formed the basis of the rules followed today. The St. Andrews club also made the historic decision to include 18 **holes** in a **round** of golf.

By this time, golf had spread into England, and a few players in North America had taken up the game as well. Evidence suggests that South Carolina was the site of the first golf in North America, but the continent's first permanent golf club was the Royal Montreal Golf Club in Canada.

Golfing rules throughout the world are regulated by two organizations: the Royal and Ancient Golf Club (R & A) and the United States Golf Association (USGA). The USGA rules over golf in America, and the R & A rules over the game everywhere else.

In 1888, a transplanted Scotsman named John G. Reid settled in Yonkers, New York. One February day, he gathered with some friends in a cow pasture and laid out three short holes, using one of his clubs to dig out the **cups**. In doing so, Reid founded the prestigious St. Andrews Golf Club, an event generally regarded as the official beginning of American golf.

holes *sets of teeing grounds, fairways, greens, and cups; most courses have 18 holes*

round *a game of golf; a round generally consists of 18 holes*

cups *the small holes into which a golfer attempts to hit the ball*

Golf took root in the U.S. with the founding of such clubs as Augusta National Golf Course.

Balls and Clubs

The first golf balls were made of wood. In the early 1600s, a new kind of ball called a feathery was made by tightly packing boiled feathers into a leather sack. Finally, around 1848, the **gutta-percha** ball was invented. Commonly called "gutties," these balls were cheap and durable, and they quickly replaced featheries as the most commonly used ball.

Featheries were very hard to make; even the most skilled feathery maker could produce only about four in a day. And even though they flew a good distance, featheries became useless when wet and quickly lost their shape.

In 1898, American golfer Coburn Haskell made a new ball by wrapping rubber threads tightly around a rubber core and covering the whole works with a hard **synthetic gum** painted white. Although ball manufacturers have made slight modifications over the years, the structure of most modern golf balls is basically the same as that created by Haskell.

Like golf balls, the first golf clubs were made entirely of wood—usually ash or hickory. The handle was sometimes wrapped in leather for a better grip. In the late 1700s, club builders began attaching iron **heads**

called cleats onto shafts. Finally, in the early 1900s, steel shafts came into use, which made clubs much stronger and more durable.

There are two basic types of golf clubs: woods and irons. Woods have longer shafts and bigger heads and are used to hit the ball a great distance. Players use them when hitting the ball off ground that is relatively smooth. For centuries, the heads of most woods were made of ash or hickory, but today most woods have steel or **titanium** heads.

In the early days of golf, players carried their clubs under their arms as they walked around the course. Golf bags for carrying clubs weren't invented until the 1870s.

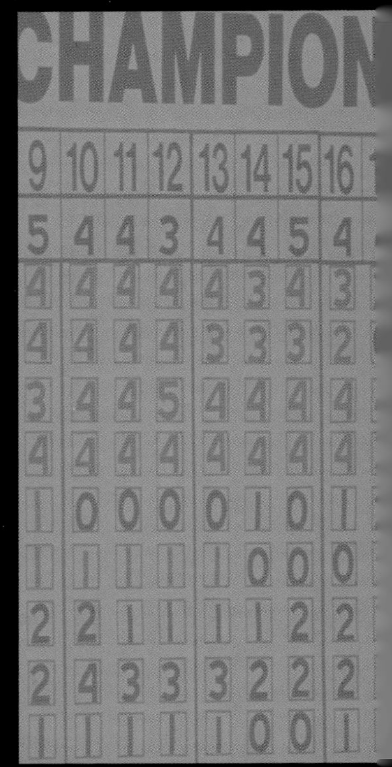

gutta-percha *a milky substance from certain tropical trees that becomes very hard after it is boiled and allowed to cool*

synthetic gum *a plastic-like substance that is hard and resists cuts or cracking*

heads *the blocky striking surfaces at the end of golf club shafts*

MOST WOODS BUILT TODAY HAVE BROAD, HOLLOW HEADS MADE OF TITANIUM OR OTHER HARD METALS.

titanium *a metal that is stronger than steel but very light*

club face *the flat part of a club's head; it is the club face that strikes the ball*

Because they are used to hit the ball from low lies or thick grass, irons have stiff shafts.

Irons have shorter, stiffer shafts that are attached to hard metal blades instead of rounded heads. Irons are used to hit the ball out of thick grass or to make shorter shots. When an iron is swung correctly, the blade digs slightly into the earth as it hits the ball, often sending a small piece of turf, called a divot, into the air.

The United States Golf Association (USGA), the organization that sets all American golfing rules, states that a player can carry no more than 14 clubs in his or her golf bag. Most professionals carry four woods, eight irons, a wedge, and a putter.

The distance a ball flies is largely determined by the angle of the **club face**. A club face that is nearly flat will hit a ball far but low. A club face that is steeply angled will launch a ball high but not very far. Golf clubs are numbered to indicate this angle. Woods are numbered from 1 to 5, and irons from 1 to 9. The lower the number, the slighter the angle of the club face and the farther the club can hit the ball.

A 1 wood is also known as a driver. It has the lowest angle of all club faces (usually about 10 or 12 degrees) and usually is used for the first shot on a hole. The average male golfer can hit a ball about 250 yards (228 m) with a driver. Woods become smaller and shorter and have more **loft** as the number gets higher. Woods numbered 2, 3, 4, and 5 are known as fairway woods.

Irons numbered 1, 2, and 3 are called long irons because players hit the ball far and get good **roll** using them. Irons 4, 5, and 6 are called middle irons, and irons 7, 8, and 9 are

loft *the degree of slant in a club face; steeper club faces are said to have more loft*

roll *motion that makes a struck ball roll a ways after landing*

backspin *motion that makes a ball spin backwards as it flies through the air and stop quickly upon landing*

A DRIVER IS GOLF'S POWER CLUB, ENABLING A PLAYER TO COVER GREAT DISTANCE IN A SINGLE SHOT.

green fees *payments to play a round of golf; green fees vary from course to course*

driving ranges *places where golfers pay money to practice hitting golf balls*

CLUB SHAFTS VARY IN LENGTH. GENERALLY, THE HIGHER A CLUB'S NUMBER, THE SHORTER ITS SHAFT WILL BE.

called short irons. Short irons don't produce great distance, but they lob the ball high into the air and give it great **backspin**. A 1 iron may hit the ball 200 yards (183 m) or more, while a 9 iron is usually used for shots of less than 100 yards (91 m).

Even though golf is incredibly popular in Japan, most golfers never play on a real course. Because land is so scarce, courses are few and require ***green fees*** *of $300 or more for a single round of golf. Most golfers "play" on* ***driving ranges*** *instead.*

The other key clubs besides woods and irons are putters and wedges. Putters have a club face that is completely flat and are used simply to roll the ball into the cup from a short distance. Wedges are like irons and have club faces that are steeply angled. They're used to hit the ball out of pockets of sand or to lob the ball close to the cup from a short distance.

Golf Courses

Golf courses are designed to be both beautiful and challenging. They can be found all over the world—in mountains, deserts, forests, alongside oceans, and even in the Arctic circle. Although each has its own distinct look and challenges, all golf courses share the same basic layout.

In 1971, when astronaut Alan B. Shepard landed on the moon, he brought golf balls and a 6 iron with him. Even though his bulky space suit limited him to short, one-handed swings, the low gravity on the moon allowed him to hit a 200-yard (183 m) shot.

Every hole on a golf course has a starting place called a teeing ground; a small patch of land called the green, which contains the cup; an unobstructed stretch of land called the fairway, which runs from the teeing ground to the green; and thick grass and various obstacles called hazards along the route to the green.

Golfers take their first shot on each hole from the teeing area. Players put the ball on a wooden or plastic peg called a tee to elevate it. They then use their driver (or sometimes a higher-numbered club if the hole is short) to drive the ball onto the fairway or the green.

hole in one *a rare feat in which a player hits the ball into the cup from the teeing ground; also called an ace*

pin *a stick with a small flag to show the location of a hole's cup; also called a flagstick*

THIS CHALLENGING HOLE FORCES GOLFERS TO LAND THEIR SHOT ON A GREEN SURROUNDED BY WATER.

On long holes, players usually try to land their first shot on the fairway, which leads to the green. Some fairways are straight. Others are laid out at an angle called a dogleg. All have closely mown grass that offers golfers a good lie, or position from which to hit their next shot.

Unless a golfer is a professional, his or her chances of making a ***hole in one*** *are about 1 in 12,600. The oldest known person to have hit a hole in one was a man named Otto Bucher, who aced a hole in 1985 at the age of 95.*

At the end of the fairway lies the green. The grass on a green is extremely short and dense, and balls roll across it easily. Somewhere on the green is the cup, a hole that is four and one-quarter inches (11 cm) in diameter and several inches deep and has a **pin** centered in it.

Hazards and **rough** add to the challenge of a hole. Hazards include pockets of sand, called sand traps or bunkers, and water in the form of ponds, streams, or even oceans. Balls hit into sand traps may be partly buried and difficult to hit out, while balls hit into water hazards are usually lost and force players to add a **penalty stroke** to their score. Holes may also have dense groups of trees running alongside the fairway.

Most courses have a **par** of 72. Each individual hole on a course also has a par, which is usually determined by distance. The distance from the teeing ground to the cup on any given hole may range from 100 to 600 yards (91–549 m). Short holes usually have a par of 3, while long holes have a par of 5. If a player finishes a hole in the same number of strokes as par, he is said to have made par. One stroke over par is a bogey, and one stroke under par is a birdie.

The longest recorded drive on a standard golf course was made by professional Michael Hoke Austin, who hit a ball a whopping 515 yards (471 m) during the U.S. Senior Open Championship in 1974.

Perhaps the most famous golf course in the world is the Old Course at St. Andrews in Scotland. Although this course has virtually no trees, its high grass and very deep bunkers make it extraordinarily challenging. Two other famous courses are found in America: Augusta National Golf Course, in Georgia, and Pebble Beach Golf Links, situated along the California coastline. Augusta is noted for its numerous water hazards and pine trees, while Pebble Beach is known for its crashing surf and stiff ocean breeze.

rough *thick grass that often flanks fairways and greens and is difficult to hit a ball from*

penalty stroke *a stroke added to a golfer's score when he violates the rules or hits the ball into certain areas*

par *the number of strokes a good golfer can be expected to hit to complete a hole or course*

Low-lying sand traps are often positioned right next to greens to add an element of difficulty.

Hitting the Ball

Although skilled players make hitting a golf ball look easy, it can be deceptively difficult. "Golf is assuredly a mystifying game," golfing legend Bobby Jones Jr. once said. "It would seem that if a person has hit a golf ball correctly a thousand times, he should be able to duplicate the performance at will. But such is certainly not the case."

Once a ball has been teed up at the start of a hole, it cannot be touched, except with clubs, until it is in the cup. The only exceptions to this rule are on the green, where a player can pick up and clean a dirty ball or remove it from the path of another golfer's putt attempt.

To hit a golf ball, a golfer grasps the club's handle with his right hand just below his left, both thumbs pointing down the shaft. (Note that these descriptions are for right-handed golfers and should be reversed for left-handers.) The player then addresses the ball, or gets in position to hit it. He extends the club until the head is just behind the ball. His feet should be about shoulder-width apart, knees slightly bent, with the ball nearly an equal distance from each foot.

Usually, the invisible line that extends from the front of one foot to the front of the other points in the direction the golfer wants the ball to go. Such a stance is said to be "square." But sometimes a player may want the ball to curve in the air to get around trees or to follow a dogleg. If a player wants to "hook" the ball, or make it curve to the left, he may pull his right foot back slightly in a "closed" stance. If a player wants to "slice" the ball, or make it curve to the right, he may pull his left foot back slightly in an "open" stance.

Golf is sometimes referred to as a "gentleman's sport" and has a number of basic rules known as etiquette. Golfers often play in groups of four. After a group has teed off, the player who is "out," or has the ball farthest from the cup, hits first.

A POWERFUL AND ACCURATE SHOT REQUIRES A STILL HEAD AND PROPER ROTATION OF THE HIPS AND SHOULDERS.

TO BLAST THE BALL FROM A BUNKER, A GOLFER USES A POWERFUL SWING TO DRIVE THROUGH THE SAND.

To start his swing, the golfer sweeps the club upward and back, away from the ball. This is called the backswing. As the club moves back, the golfer shifts his weight onto his back foot and turns his upper torso. At the top of the backswing, the golfer's hands should be above his right ear with the club shaft nearly parallel to the ground. The shoulders and waist are twisted, coiling the body like a spring.

The player then shifts his weight back to his front foot, pivots his hips, and brings the club back down to strike the ball. As the club face hits the ball, the arms continue to carry the club through the swing in a sweeping motion. Throughout the swing,

Golfers should make sure other players are out of range before hitting. If a player hits a ball in the direction of other golfers, he or she should yell out the traditional warning, "Fore!"

To make it to the top of the leader board, competitive golfers need a well-balanced game.

even as the golfer's waist and shoulders rotate, his head should remain still. This is perhaps the single most important factor in hitting a golf ball consistently well.

The above description explains the basic swing for "full" shots with woods and long irons. Pitches and chips are short shots in which a golfer uses a partial swing to hit the ball onto the green. A pitch is a lofted shot with a wedge or short iron that puts backspin on the ball so that it

Many golfers wear special golf shoes on the course. The shoes have small spikes in the bottom to give the golfer better traction when hitting. Some players also wear a glove to give them a better grip on the club.

stops quickly after landing. A chip is a low shot with a middle or long iron that doesn't rise high into the air but rolls a ways after landing.

The other main swing in golf is the **putt**. There is a saying that golfers "drive for show but putt for dough." In other words, a 300-yard (274 m) drive looks impressive, but players tend to improve their scores most by getting better at putting. When putting, a golfer keeps the blade of the putter close to the turf of the green and makes a short, even stroke. The putting stroke should resemble the pendulum swing of a clock, with the head of the putter moving the same distance backward as forward.

According to golf rules, a player must add a stroke to his score even if he swings at the ball and misses it. If a player hits his ball but can't find it after the shot, he must add a penalty stroke to his score and hit a new ball from the same place he hit the last one.

putt *a very short shot on the green in which a player taps the ball and rolls it toward the cup*

THE SPIKES IN GOLF SHOES GIVE PLAYERS BETTER TRACTION, ESPECIALLY AS THEY HIT FROM UNEVEN GROUND.

Professional Golf

Golf has long been a major professional sport. Today, men's pro golf is regulated by the Professional Golfers Association (PGA), an organization founded in 1916. A corresponding organization for women—the Ladies' Professional Golfers Association (LPGA)—was established in 1950.

Golf etiquette requires players to be quiet when other players are preparing for a shot; to replace divots in the ground and stamp them down; and to allow faster golfers to "play through," or pass them, on the golf course.

There are many professional men's tournaments worldwide, but the four most famous ones are the British Open, the U.S. Open, the PGA Championship, and the Master's Tournament. Collectively, these tournaments are known as "the majors." **Amateurs** as well as professionals play in both opens. The top tournaments for professional women are the Ladies' British Open, the U.S. Women's Open, and the LPGA Championship. In most pro tournaments, each golfer plays four rounds, or 72 holes.

The first great men's golfers hailed from Scotland. In the mid-1800s,

a feathery manufacturer named Allan Robertson was considered the world's best golfer. That title soon went to Tom Morris Jr., who won four British Opens by the age of 21 and became the most revered figure in the history of Scottish golf. In the 1890s, England began producing some of the world's best players, including John Henry Taylor and Harry Vardon.

A shot made from a sand trap is called a recovery shot. A golfer uses a wedge or a short iron, takes a wide stance, and hits the sand an inch or two behind the ball. If hit correctly, the ball will fly from the bunker in an explosion of sand.

Two of the first American stars were Bobby Jones Jr. and Gene Sarazen. The fiery Jones, who played as an amateur and for only eight years, compiled 13 combined victories in

TIGER WOODS COMPLETED THE CAREER GRAND SLAM (WINNING ALL FOUR MAJORS) BY THE AGE OF 24.

amateurs *golfers who play for recreation or trophies but not money*

the U.S. and British Open and Amateur championships. In 1930, he won all four events in the same year, an incredible feat known as the "Grand Slam" of golf during that era.

In the 1940s, American Ben Hogan rose to the top of the golfing world. In 1949, he was nearly killed in a car accident. The quiet but steely Hogan was back on the course a year later, however, and won the British Open, the U.S. Open, and the Masters in 1953. He was succeeded by Arnold Palmer, perhaps the world's greatest golfer in the 1950s and '60s. In the decades that followed, Jack Nicklaus, Tom Watson, and Lee Trevino also earned places among the all-time greats.

But the player that many golf fans believe will go down as the greatest of all time came along in the mid-1990s. That player was Tiger Woods. From 1994 to 1996, Woods captured the U.S. Amateur championship every year, prompting Jack Nicklaus to say, "Arnold [Palmer] and I both agreed that you could take his Masters and my Masters and add them together [a total of 10 trophies], and this kid should win more than that."

Woods was an instant star when he turned professional in 1997 at age 21. In his first pro season, he won the Masters by a tournament-record 12 strokes. Woods embodied the ultimate combination of power and precision, sending 350-yard (320 m) drives rocketing down fairways and sinking seemingly impossible putts. His success triggered increased interest in the sport among young people and minority players.

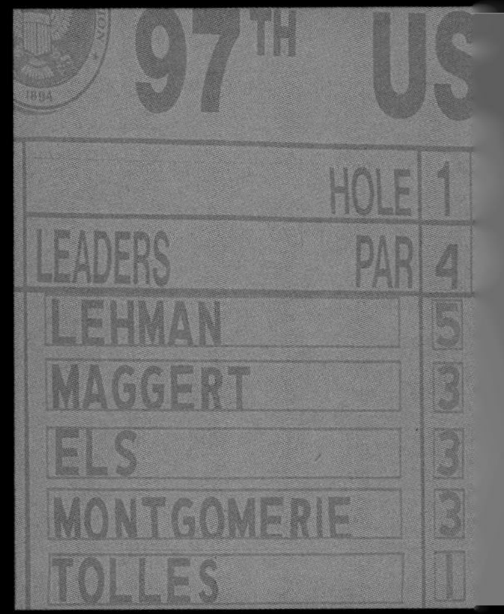

In 2001, Annika Sorenstam shot a tournament round of 59—the lowest in the history of women's golf.

Women's professional golf has also produced many legendary players, beginning with British amateurs Lady Margaret Scott and Dorothy Campbell in the 1890s. Perhaps no British golfer, however, was better than Joyce Wethered. With her uncanny concentration and sweet swing, Wethered won four British Amateur titles in the 1920s. "I have not played with anyone, man or woman, amateur or professional, who made me feel so utterly outclassed," the great Bobby Jones Jr. once said of Wethered.

The first golf tournament to be broadcast on national television was May's World Championship in 1953. Tournament organizers paid ABC $32,000 to have the event telecast. Soon, such dealings were reversed; television networks began paying to air the events.

The women's game took firm hold in the United States after World War I. One of America's first stars was Mildred "Babe" Didrikson Zaharias, a tremendous athlete and former Olympian known for her towering tee shots. Succeeding Zaharias were

Mickey Wright, Kathy Whitworth, and Nancy Lopez, all Americans who helped to build up women's golf from the 1960s to the '80s. In the 1990s, several women outside of North America dominated the game. These included Britain's Laura Davies, Sweden's Annika Sorenstam, and Australia's Karrie Webb.

By the start of the 21st century, both men's and women's professional golf enjoyed huge popularity. Enormous galleries flanked the holes of every major pro tournament, with the PGA's annual prize money totaling close to $100 million and the LPGA Tour paying out more than $30 million a year. But golf is still—and always will be—played most widely by recreational golfers who may never master the game but cannot resist its allure.

The lowest score ever recorded on an 18-hole course in a major golf tournament was a 55, shot in 1962 by a 24-year-old named Homero Blancas in the Premier Invitational. The average male golfer shoots a score in the high 90s.

PRO GOLF INVOLVES BIG MONEY AND GALLERIES, BUT AT ITS CORE, GOLF IS A QUIET GAME OF PERSONAL CHALLENGE.

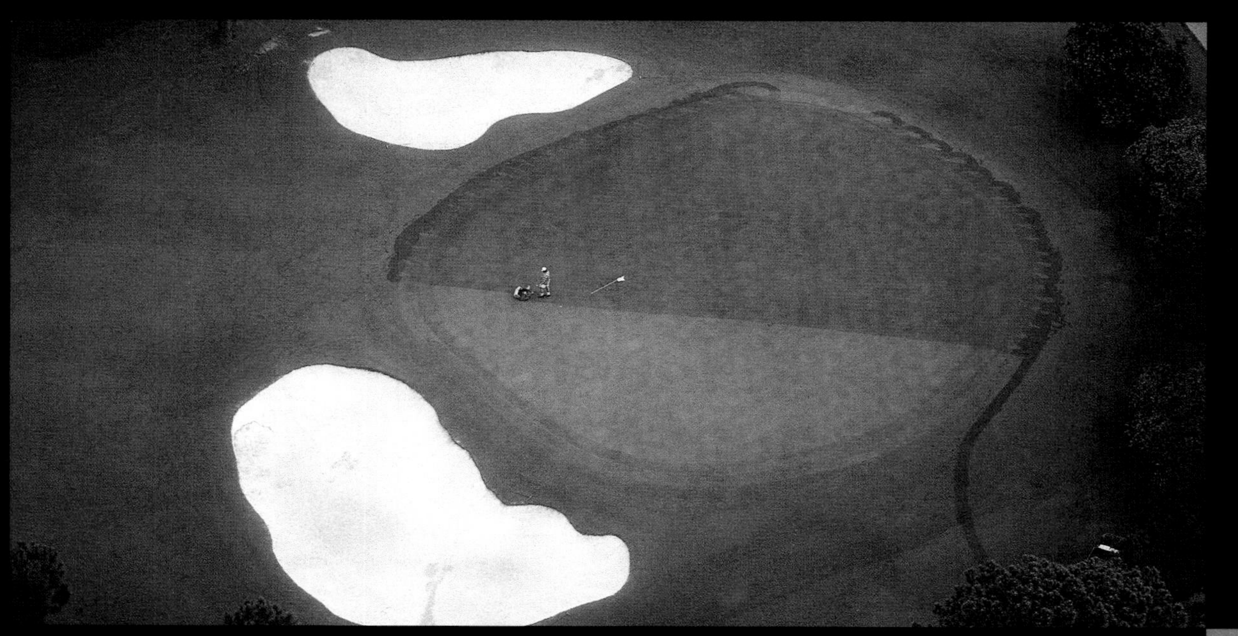

INDEX

GLEN ROCK PUBLIC LIBRARY, NJ
3 9110 05050097 6